The
Weak
One
Was
Him

A story of ultimate betrayal

by

Deborah Rosa Jimenez

All the information contained in this book is based on the life experiences and opinions perceived and expressed by the author.

No part of this book may be reproduced or transmitted in any form or by any means electronically or mechanically, including photocopying or recording without prior written consent by the author or the publisher.

This book is printed in the United States.

Publisher:

Rose Gold Publishing, LLC
www.rosegoldpublishingllc.com

ISBN - 13: 978-1-7332638-0-1
ISBN - 10: 1-7332638-0-2

iv

Disclaimer:

The stories shared in this book are raw and contain adult content and language.

This book is not for children.

The deliberate and intentional content allows the reader to understand what domestic violence can do to a person and what it did to the author.

There are many forms of domestic violence including physical, sexual, verbal, emotional and financial.

Remember, you are not alone and no one has the right to hurt you.

Domestic Violence Hotline: 800-799-7233

Steps for securing a restraining order, are shared at the back of the book.

The
Weak
One
Was
Him

A story of ultimate betrayal

by

Deborah Rosa Jimenez

TABLE OF CONTENTS

About the Author

Deborah Rosa Jimenez is 52 years old, a mother of a son; Andres and two grandsons, Gabriel, and AJ. She is the baby girl of 4 siblings. (She loves them all! - Milly, Sandra, Maritza, and Jose!)

She is a Land and Water Fitness Instructor and also a nanny.

She wrote this book to express her rage and to heal from Domestic Abuse that she personally experienced at this age.

Domestic violence is often not addressed. Very often because it's emotional or verbal, even financial. It led her to one physical incident that was more than enough for her. She soon realized you can't change people, but you don't have to accept their abusive behavior either.

She is neither bitter nor regretful, but she is definitely wiser. She too encourages others to have their voices be heard. *#maybehedoesnthityou* is real.

You will find information regarding assistance if you have found yourself in a domestic abuse situation, especially if your abuser won't leave. Use it.

Use your voice and get your power back.
This is her story.

She may reached at theweakonewashim@gmail.com or https://www.facebook.com/Maybehedoesnthityou-1159498627538820/.

It was Sunday, 6/24/18.

A beautiful summer, sunny, breezy day.
That day my abuser called the sheriff on me! Two days before I had that same department throw him the fuck out.

This was the day I knew the entire relationship was a game. Nothing was real.

Nothing, but the immense pain that I felt.

It was a beautiful lie

I wished I died inside

so, I'd bypass the cries

collide with my rage

I felt caged

I turn the crumpled page…

#maybehedoesnthityou   (maybe he doesn't hit you)

But what else does he do?
Laugh at you?
Try to shame you?
Say you're cuckoo?
Saying it's you?
Running the game,
placing all blame
directly on you

No matter what you do.
Scatterbrain, neurotic
asking if you are psychotic
An emotional accident, what?
Just stop what the fuck!!!

A good little victim he says,
he's fucked up all in his head
from a man that acts legit,
but the boy seriously turned out to be shit

Next comes the physical
you got to do what's logical, take off
Throw out the trash! Do something rash.

The arrogance he displays
will be wiped off his fucken face
The satisfaction that you feel
will help your deceived heart heal.
"...names will never hurt you"

is a lie broken
people can cut you,
that's their cry.
Watch these mother fucking mouths
aimed at you.
Maybe he doesn't hit you,
but what else does he do?

Dorian Gray

He reminds me of "The Picture of Dorian Gray."
Fabulous to look at
yet actually shriveled and frayed

That's what his heart appears to be
for the dirty mother fucking way he did me

I'm working thru anger I have to let him go
I ain't dealing with him grabbing me!
HELL NO!

Talking to me any kind of way
I gave him a home, and I got played.

He forgot one thing
I'm not really weak
I'm a mother fuckin Alpha
I'll get on my feet!

He'll be a distant memory very soon
I won't see his shadows in my bedroom
He is doomed
Cyanide.
Cuz Midnight?
He died.

☠ Murdered by ego, meanness, and lies
Arrogance and bullshit
Nope not my type

He reminds me of "The Picture of Dorian Gray."
Not really handsome
But shriveled and frayed.

Game Over

You're mad because you
underestimated me
wish I had seen your face
when the sheriffs came for you
the anger, the shame?

You felt some kind of way
because you bit the hand
of the one who loved you all the way
to the moon and back
and you're going to steal from ME?!

You must have been manic
past due time to set you free
yelled at me, gaslight fail
thank God for my kids
I would have gone to jail
no bail
you're a fail

and your mask fell to the ground
I don't want you around
warning label
this bitch is a fable

no integrity
he hides it from 8 to 3
acting like he is the smartest around
tons of info

but this man's a clown
not down
for anyone not even himself

All info no wisdom
his stability is shelved
a user
a loser
a dreamer
a schemer
with low self-esteem
he wants to be the dream
of every woman around

but he will just astound you
with the putridness inside
he tries to hide from the pain
that resides
silent cries

insular my ass
quite abrasive from his past
he will say that he is woke
his Amenra's a fucking joke
he chokes on his inconsistency

Did you really think I couldn't set me free?
hee hee, you see how very wrong you are
looking pretty stupid
and thank you for the car.

He Was an Abuser

My grip was so tight around the knife that the white of my knuckles could be seen.

He was on his knees; a knife plunged deep in the side of his neck.

I was mesmerized as I stared at my hand, blood now dripping on it too.

I snapped out of it and immediately began crying uncontrollably.

It was in that moment; I knew that abuser had TO GO.

ABUSER—I realized; he was an abuser.

The rage I felt was so intense, it terrified me that I could harbor such viciousness.

FUCK YOU LETTER

Dearest Dark-heart:

I wanted to express how much I hate your fucken ass at this moment, the taste is so disgustingly bad!

HAHA fuck you bitch the judge gave me MY car. You don't give shit to people and then take it back when it suits your feelings, pendejo!

That was such satisfaction seeing the shock on your face when you realized you weren't getting the van back.

How fucken dare you even think to put a finger on me! What the fuck is wrong with you!? Hard enough to bruise me! Yes, you did look surprised in court, but that doesn't change shit.

You grabbed me and hurt me you fucken sucio. The day you called the cops on me too. What kind of lowlife, classless shit is that?

You and I both know, I have always been good to you, right back to when we were just friends.

I realize you love the way I love you, but you have no love for me. A man would not subject someone he truly loves to this bullshit. You fucken underestimated me, you stupid fucker! I loved you like crazy, but I loved me

MORE! I will not forget the look on your pregnant daughters' face, having to come to terms with what a lowlife her own father is despite all his shit talking. You looked like a fucken idiot when I said in court if anything like this happened to any one of your daughters you would be pounding on the guy's door to hit his face. You going to yell out; damn right! Were you drunk?

You looked like an idiot and confirmed all I said. All those lies about me abusing you. How fucken dare you? Bitch! You were abusive right after you steadily started working. Always trying to fight about stupid shit.

Had me stumped! You didn't stump the judge. You weren't "believable" cuz it was all bullshit, and she saw thru it! Thank God! I promise you; you will remember me for the rest of your life!

It took courage and loving the shit out of myself to get you thrown out! The plus for me, it was on your mother's birthday! I hope every year you recall what a piece of shit you were to me and learn from your fuckups. Not this woman motherfucker!

I also now know that your so-called best friend is your woman now. Low class! Disgusting! I panicked after thinking WTF and I had every STD test available done on me. Thank God all was good!
You will surely reap what you sow. You are a perfect example of being comfortable in your discomfort. After

all, what kind of a real man would be abusing a woman that has always had his back? Fuck you!

Maybe you had to be reminded of what it is to be loved, and perhaps I had to learn unconditional love. I did that and wished while I'm typing this letter, I didn't have love for you, but you better believe, I love me more. Fuck you and all your bullshit! Your oldest daughter was right! "You will hurt every woman you come across until you heal yourself!"

Good luck! You'll need it, little bitch!

Ever so fucking sincerely,

Deborah Rosa Jimenez

HOSPITALIZED

I had been feeling run down for a while. He finally began to work in March, but things felt different I could recall telling him to shut the fuck up because of the manner he was speaking to my grandson. Little did I know that was the tip of the iceberg of his hatefulness overflowing onto others.

My grandson was playing doctor at our house one day and went up to him and said, let me check you. I heard him laugh saying "How you are going to give me a checkup, and you don't look healthy" I came out of my room and said he's perfectly healthy, don't talk to my grandson that way. I'm sure the look of daggers I was giving him, he felt…

Later I told him, don't you dare ever speak to my grandson negatively. If your childhood was riddled with adults that insulted you, that is something YOU need to get over.

You see, I knew his family called him ugly, blackie, stupid, saying he's too skinny and tall, among other things. He looked at me and apologized and said I was right. He didn't realize it. I calmed down and told him, it sounds like you still need to get over your childhood. This was the week before I was hospitalized.

On April 30th, I was hospitalized for a fever that lasted three days and a migraine that made me weep in the dark. I came home from a Zumba gold class and went to bed. I could not sleep, my fever wouldn't go away, and my head was making me nauseous.

I have an autoimmune disorder, lupus, which stress markers make so much worse. This was the case for me.

I finally decided to go to the hospital. He was in the living room as I called out to him; he didn't hear me or pretended not to. I told him to take me to the emergency room; looking back; he was more bothered than concerned.

Once we arrived at the hospital, I could recall him saying, "I'm going outside, you know how much I hate hospitals," as I waited for triage. Wow.

I was admitted to the hospital that day. I endured so many tests to try to find the source of infection, making my fever return consistently.

There were moments where he let me lay on his lap, stroking my head, and I was grateful.

There was another moment that was a first though. It was the first time I wanted him to leave. He conveniently had to leave the hospital as I was waiting to be taken to my room. His vibe was off to me, but I dismissed it, I just did not feel well.

The second day I was in the hospital, he called me very early and told me he couldn't find our van. He sounded baffled and irritated. I asked him where he parked it, and as he answered, he was obviously so annoyed with me. I recall telling him he didn't have to be so nasty it wasn't my fault. He stated he was just trying to figure out what had happened. When I questioned the position of the car, he said he backed up into the parking space. A move that is not allowed in our complex. We had this discussion before when I got towed nearly a year ago for that very reason. I questioned how could he not recall that? It was the same week my bank account was hacked! We had numerous discussions. Was he just not paying attention to what I was saying? He called the towing company, and sure enough, the car was towed!

So, I'm in the hospital, they still don't know what is wrong, my fever is constant, my migraine is too, and now I have to deal with the irate cursing and the gaslight of an asshole.

He yelled at me; he said this isn't about the world picking on me; he messaged me to "not text or call him. He's "tired of fighting with me," " no one's good for you but you," "you are touched in the head," " calm the fuck down" right down to " whatever, you use the van more than I do" the messages were endless. He went so far and said, you know when you have medical issues, you always display mental problems". Yes, I kept the texts to remind me of the shit that came out of him when I needed him the most. (which was really hilarious because I don't fight; all the issues were a reaction to his words, actions or lack of).

He was horrible; I cried in the hospital in disbelief at how cruel he had been, especially when the van being towed was his fault! I decided it was over! What kind of a man is going to fight and verbally abuse someone who was just hospitalized!

I had no idea how I was going to go back to taking 27 to 32 buses and trains to get to my classes and babysitting jobs. I had no idea how I was going to make up for the time I was hospitalized and missing work. I just knew I didn't want to be with someone that could be so cruel when I was so ill, and the doctors still hadn't figured out what was wrong.

The next day he came to visit as if nothing were wrong. I recall him saying you know how much I hate to see a woman crying. He was the sweetest of the sweetest. Was stroking my head to relax me and telling me not to worry about anything. The entire time I thought WTF this man was a demon yesterday! What the fuck is going on!? I didn't have the energy to put into it and just wanted to let it go, but my words rang in my head from the previous day.

We're finished you mean ass motherfucker! I don't want a man that can be that cruel. Later, I thought how I should've stuck to this decision after he so nastily said, "you like to be sick, play the good little victim" …

When it was time to leave the hospital, it was my sister who picked me up.

4 MINUTES

Four minutes, four minutes. I could not stop repeating this phrase in my head. My teeth were clenched, and my hands were wrapped around the steering wheel as if my life depended on it. What the fuck was wrong with this motherfucker!?? I should've fucken stuck to the decision I made in the hospital to leave him! Little did I know the hospital was the beginning of the end.

We shared a car, and I was supposed to pick him up after work at 3 pm. I was driving from Des Plaines to Chicago, and traffic was heavier than expected. I thought, hmmm I might be late, so I sent a quick text saying I'd be 5-10 minutes late. He replies, "are you serious? Wtf." I chose not to respond, wondering why did he react that way? I was a half block away from his job, and there he was, California and Granville.

I pulled over after the light and could see his face looking straight demonic as he came around to the driver's side; 6 ft 9 inches of rage emitting such hate. My naivety hadn't prepared me for the abuse that was coming.

He walked around to the driver's side and opened the door. I said no, that's ok, I'll drive. He then slammed the van door with such force that I began to shake, and my fingernails poked into the palms of my hands. I'm trying to calm a flood of rage I could feel from the pit of my stomach. The force of the slam shook the van. I turned towards the passenger seat looking at him incredulously, saying what THE FUCK is wrong with you! You didn't need to slam that door like you're having a tantrum! He immediately starts screaming, I let you use my car, and you can't even make it on time! What the fuck is wrong with you!

This was the first time he called the van his. I looked over at the bright light illuminated on the clock, 3:04 pm. I stared- 4 minutes; you are tripping like this over 4 minutes? He said, let's go, drive, and he continued to talk shit. "I work with kids all day when 3 pm hits I wanna be the fuck outta there! I don't wanna hang out or talk; I wanna get the fuck out!"

A slew of profanities continued as I felt the situation was so surreal. I was shocked…I suddenly heard the putrid bullshit spewing out of his mouth towards me as I drove, I turned to him and screamed Shut the fuck up!

He grabbed the keys from the ignition and suddenly turned the car off as I was driving across Granville. Yelling, he doesn't want a psycho bitch driving him! I nearly hit another vehicle. He literally snatched the key as I was driving. I was fast and snatched the keys when they were barely out of the ignition, put them back in the ignition and started the van and yelled with the craziest of rage. Fuck you! I'm driving!

I could see the shock on his face. Who the fuck do you think you are? Don't be screaming at me! I drove to

Des Plaines, gripping the steering wheel so hard I bruised my palm. My mind was racing. He proceeded to get on the phone to chat with whoever as if nothing happened. I sat fuming. Could not believe it. I should've stuck to my decision when I was in the hospital two weeks ago. I wanted that man out of my life.

It was the beginning of the end.

4 minutes, 4minutes. I could not stop repeating this phrase in my head. My teeth were clenched, and my hands were wrapped around the steering wheel as if my life depended on it.

He later asked me why I was making such a big deal about a little thing. You can't let shit go…

As I replayed that bullshit in my mind, I still could not believe it. WTF is wrong with him!

DRUNK PUNK

I recall that Friday, 06/22/18, I was off, but he had to go to work. I woke up and went to the kitchen, and boy was he in a hell of a mood.

Good morning.

He responded; you think?

I said someone is in a bad mood, take it with you. If you don't want to talk, just say that, and I grabbed some coffee and went back to get ready to take him to work.

I'd was using the car for errands. That day he got paid, and he was to supposed to give me $600 for the rent that we were already behind. When I asked him for it, he was so offended. Calm down; I'm going to give it to you.   I told him he didn't have to be so fucken nasty. He knew what he had to do. I said I wanted it before I dropped him off because I was going to give the landlord a check. He grudgingly complied and said ok since everything always has to be your way. I bit my tongue, whatever.

I drove over to California and Devon, where there was a Capitol one ATM. He came back and gave me money, I counted $200. I said, are you crazy? I need $400 more. He said he couldn't take more out of the ATM. I told him he's full of shit and he's just going to be late because I wasn't moving.

This man got out of the car walking back to the bank with his arm raised fully in the air giving me the finger. Un-fucken-believable. He came back with $200 and said he'd have to take out the rest later. I took it and told him how irresponsible he is. I dropped him off at work and left. The next day he would wait until I was furious to give me the rest of the money while laughing.

That afternoon when I picked him up, I could smell the liquor on his breath. It was 3 pm. I don't even recall what putridness he was on; I asked what is wrong? He said nothing, why don't you go find somebody or something to do and leave me alone. I said wow you're mean; I don't know you and don't want to know you anymore. I proceeded to drive home with music on.

When we got back home, I pointed to the door and said, or you could leave me alone, I don't need anyone that's so fucken mean.

I proceeded to watch a movie in my bedroom and fell asleep.

That next morning, Sat 6/23. I was going to pick up my grandson. We had discussed this earlier in the week, and I reminded him the previous day.

This was the first time he manipulated the use of the van that was supposed to be mine. In retrospect, he wanted his name on the title too. How foolish was I? I did ask why, after all, he bought it for me. At the time he had a truck. As I was getting ready, he asked where I was going. I reminded him I was picking up my grandson. I also reminded him there was a party at my niece's house, which we had already agreed I was taking the van. I told him, by the way, I revoke the invite because there's no way my family is meeting a motherfucker like you!

It turned into oh man; I was going to Maywood to visit my daughters - blah, blah blah- in such a manner I was disgusted with him. I said how about I go pick up my grandson, and you take the car and all your shit and stay there. I don't like the aggressive shitty way you're talking to me.

He laughed and said he just might do that. I said okay because if you're so miserable you have to put it on me, get the fuck out. Oh, you are throwing me out. I said no, you're throwing yourself out! I can't stand how mean you are being; it makes me want to smack the fuck out of you. He laughed some more. I left to pick my grandson up and sent him a text letting him know not to come out with his bullshit when I arrive with my grandson. His response ...

"Eat shit you dramatic emotional accident waiting to happen...if I am such a shit, why do you want me; stop texting me; you scattered brain neurotic fucken cup of coffee" I responded you should've respected me! I told him I realized he's a loser and an emotional abuser. I told him I need a man, not a little bitch!

He responded, 'Eat a dick". I told him I understood now that what his daughter said about never leaving her child with him was not a joke. He responded, "eat shit and worry about your own," I replied, you should've respected me, especially now!

I' was always good to you. I told him it was hard to swallow who he really was, that he had no integrity and he should leave. I told him he would never hear from me again. No response. I knew I wasn't going to be able to go to my niece's family party. I was livid. On the exterior, I was cool because I was getting my grandson. He had just begun summer vacation, and I was not going to let this monster dim my joy.

When I returned a few hours later, he was just as obnoxious as ever. I again said, please take your shit, I'll figure out how to get my grandson home tomorrow. He went out the door laughing. I was annoyed beyond belief and just sat my ass down and carried on with my grandson. At this point, my plans to go out changed since I didn't have a car. My grandson played with the neighbor's kids and ran around having a good time while I watched; my heart was smiling.

I recalled how phony he had sounded to me the day I came home from the hospital. "Miss you, baby, I'm glad you are home" I was laying on the couch watching him in the kitchen and thought I don't know about this.

That Saturday afternoon, I had hoped he wouldn't return. His vibe was so vicious, so mocking, so toxic... The day had progressed smoothly, filled with laughter and fun. My grandson and I had eaten dinner, and we were going to watch a movie. He calls, and the thought of not picking up crossed my mind, I had never felt that way. I picked up and he so lovingly asked if Gabriel and I had eaten dinner. I said yes, and he had some in the microwave. He said he'll be there later than. I just said, ok.

An hour later, here comes this evil ass clearly drunk. Walks in talking about did you even feed the boy, what kind of grandmother are you...I immediately got up from the sofa and went up to him and said seriously? Why did they even let you leave Maywood driving this drunk? You should've stayed there. Again, you are putting me out. I said if you're going to just talk negative shit to cause trouble yes. He laughed and left. I thought that was the end of that, but no.

About an hour later, my grandson was playing in the bedroom; he was exhausted from the day. I could hear some loud music that sounded like it was by my door, but after all, it was summertime and had been a beautiful sunny day. I went to my back door and looked out an open window. Perfect timing. I heard him on the phone asking some woman to call him, and that he missed her. I was amazed. What the fuck! I went back inside and was furious. This motherfucker is sitting in the back of our home calling some other chick. Bitch no! I was done!

My grandson fell asleep, and I laid on the sofa to watch TV, hoping this motherfucker would leave. I double locked all the doors, although he had keys.

So here comes this man two hours later. Walks up to me in the living room and asks what are you doing here? I'm sprawled out on one of the sofas and sit up and said, what the fuck do you mean, I live here! He says you are trying to lock me out. I said I know you have keys I thought if I made it hard enough, you'd just leave. He laughed and said, I'll leave when I'm ready to go. I must've given him the dirtiest look ever. You don't love me anymore, laughing. I looked at him and said, I love you. I just don't like how mean you are being and the way you talk to me.

A few minutes later he's sitting at the table and talking shit because I'm in the living room where he is going to sleep. I said too fucken bad, why don't you have the bitch you calling pick you up? I'll help you take your shit out. He looked genuinely surprised, but he was also drunk. I get up and go over to where he's sitting and tell him why don't you just leave? He said hoe, please!

With no thought whatsoever, my hand landed across his mouth, and I busted his lip. I was just as surprised as him. I told him you may be used to dealing with hoes and bitches, but this woman doesn't deal with this bullshit. You are calling me a hoe in my house. Get out! And shut the fuck up my grandson is sleeping.! He jumped up and touched his lip and started screaming, waving his arms around, saying that he'll tear up my whole damn house if I touched him one more time. In my mind, I wanted to beat him out the fucken door. I was in total disbelief of this situation. All 6 ft 9 inches of him looked totally enraged, like a devil. I again told him to leave. He said he wasn't going anywhere and took that opportunity to plop himself on the sofa. I was beyond upset, I couldn't even believe I popped him in the lip, but even more incredible his calling me a hoe! I went to the bathroom and tried to call his adult daughters. Neither picked up. I left a VM asking either one of them to call their father and get him out of my house. I said I don't want to call the police, my grandson is here, and he's being totally vicious. When I got out of the bathroom, he was asleep on the sofa.

I went to my room in disbelief. I couldn't sleep. I couldn't figure out how the fuck to have this man leave of his own accord. What did he think would happen? What the fuck is wrong with him? How could he be so fucken mean?

I later went to the living room looking at him sleeping and still couldn't believe it. I thought of how the previous month he fought with me while in the hospital. I felt at that moment how this motherfucker is hindering my recovery. I thought you can't be this mean and it is the first time! This man had a mask on the whole time! It was quite a revelation.

His phone was sitting on the table. Neither of us locked our phones. It was never an issue. I sat down and went on his FB. An hour later, I would never be the same. I was meant to read all the messages I read, like some kind of confirmation that this man was never serious about me. He loved the way I loved him. That's it. I believe that more than ever now. I cried my heart out because I knew we were done. His messages showed me that he was always mean, but not to me. Messages to women he had kept in contact with, talking in the most putrid manner to his ex-wife. Times he had ignored his daughter's messages when I knew he was available. Messages that showed me I didn't know this man at all. And I no longer wanted to.

POLICE CALLED ON ME

At some point, I must've fallen asleep. I jumped up startled and sat in bed as I recalled the bullshit that had occurred the previous night. I looked over at my grandson still asleep and thought it was the perfect opportunity to see if this Midnight monster would just leave. I did not want anything going down while he's in my house. We're all about fun, and no drama just love!

I go to the living room, and there's Midnight sprawled across the sofa pretending he was asleep. I don't know how I knew, but I did.

I went up to the couch and said Gabriel is still sleeping. Why don't you just take your shit and leave? He said, you know if I leave, I'm taking my van. I said, oh your van now, huh? He said yeah, I bought it. I told him, you forgot who you bought it for. I said, you know what? Take that van and stick it up your ass, may I never see you again. You're horrible. I deserve better, and you don't deserve me. Just leave.

He laughed in my face — a menacing, loud, obnoxious, evil laugh. My stomach literally turned. He never budged from the couch and what do I see on a tv table? A cigar. I told him don't you dare light that shit in here, you know my grandson is here! He said he'll do what the fuck he wants, still laughing. Before he could grab the cigar, I grabbed it and crumbled it all over the table. Apparently, he only had one. He laughed and said I better replace that. I calmed down and asked him why he didn't just leave. I'm not gonna support his behavior. That he must've lost his fucken mind if he thought that. He said, go over there, leave me alone. WTFF! My ass was burnt up, but at the same time, I felt like he was trying to get me to fight with him. That's not my style. I was appalled I had said all the things that I said, though they were real. I have always talked to my men with respect. He totally lost mine, and I was ghetto as hell. My saving grace was that I had my grandson with me.

I walked over to a TV table against the wall where I saw his keys. I took the keys and started to look for the house keys.   He jumped off the sofa so fast and grabbed my arm, and spun me around, and he snatched the keys out of my hand as I bumped very hard into the TV table that was now behind me.

He sat on the sofa, looking satisfied with himself and said I told you, I'll leave when I'm ready. I was standing there looking at my arm as I still held it up and looked at him. You're gonna grab me over some fucken keys like that!? Are you fucken crazy motherfucker?! So many bad things went thru my mind the rage I felt that he dared to put a finger on me! I'd never done a bad thing to this man. I thought this man was my friend since we'd met in 1993! The eight or nine years I hadn't seen him indeed were becoming clear of the type of person he had become.

He jumps up and says let me just call the police before this elevates. I stood there in fucken disbelief; do you hear me! Call the police! I'm steadily telling him to leave that I didn't want to call the police and voila!

So, there you have it. He called the police on me; as so many things ran thru my head. I went to check on my grandson, and he was awake. I rushed him thru brushing his teeth, gave him fruit, and asked him if he'd like to watch a movie in bed with the headphones. Of course, he loved the idea. I told him I'm going to step outside for just a minute, not to worry I'd never leave him. He said ok, and I hugged him and told him that I loved him.

I close my bedroom door to face whatever the fuck this is going to be. My heart is pounding. I want to cry, but I'm thinking good the police will make him leave. I go to the bathroom to splash water on my face and try to stop thinking of how bad I want to beat the fuck out of this man. Who the fuck is that? Who am I!?

The sheriff's department is who comes to unincorporated Des Plaines. We both go outside, because no way this is happening in my fucken house. I tell the officer about the night before. I tell him I want him to leave. I tell him this shit can't continue my grandson is in the house. Why the fuck can't he be a man and leave?

His turn. I don't have to leave. I am a resident, I get mail here, and I would have to be evicted. I'll never forget how he looked. 6 ft 9 in, black as midnight, smoking what was left of the broken cigar, arms crossed with an evil ass smile looking at me.

It was a beautiful Sunday morning, about 10 am; the sun was shining; it was about 70 degrees. I looked at him, and in that very moment I knew this man never, ever loved me, and I got played. In that instant, every perspective changed. I looked at the officer, and he had a look on his face and said that is true. I said, but he's not on my lease. He said it doesn't matter. If he established residency, he is correct. A piece of information I never knew I needed to know! But he knew. He researched this. This entire relationship was by design. a bad, fractured bullshit design. I told the officer what if he's putting his hands on me and threatening me?
He speaks up and said, yea what do I do? Because I'm afraid for my life. I'll know what to do, and we'll have this in a report.

WHAT THE FUCK! THIS BITCH! I couldn't believe my ears. The officer looks at him and starts telling us the location at the Skokie courthouse to get an order of protection, including the process. He says good to know. The sheriff looked at me and said is there anything else you want to add? I omitted where he grabbed me to grab the keys. I don't even know why. I think I wanted to give him one more chance to leave on his own, really believing he'd take it. I told the officer no. The officer looks at both of us and said, you know you are adults. I don't want to be called back because this elevated. There's a kid in the house.

I was fucken mortified. I told the sheriff to ask him to leave of his own accord then. He said I'm not going, officer. I just paid rent, you going to give me that money back? I didn't bother to tell him how full of shit he was. The sheriff left.

I went inside checked on my grandson, and he was still watching his movie. I said I'd make breakfast for him to stay where he was. I went to the bathroom and cried like I don't recall ever crying. I was furious; I felt helpless; I felt betrayed, lost. I felt horrible. This is when I imagine stabbing him. ..

I got myself together and saw we were out of eggs. I thought this is the right time to grab my grandson and run to the store. I got my keys and knew they were lighter and realized he had taken my car keys off my keychain. I went to the living room and asked for them. He said no, that's my van. Walk. I said fuck you and walked away and made pancakes instead the entire time thinking we're getting dressed and going outside. The whole place was filled with a dark vapor of malice that I could taste like a disastrous recipe on your first try. I couldn't stand it. I felt it in my soul. Why does he feel so evil now? I was so stunned. I could recall him passing by me saying oh yea, you one of those broads that like to get beat. I said fuck you get away from me. What a shocking thing to say!

After breakfast, my grandson and I went to play outside for a couple of hours. We came in to get water and eat. It was a hot beautiful day, and he was running around on his scooter. It's so wondrous how something so fabulously beautiful could coexist in the same space as putrid evil. It was scary. All I could think of was that I needed to get my grandson home. I'm gonna have to cut his visit short. I felt even more terrible with the thought.

When we came into the house, he was all smiles and said, I thought you guys were going to the water park. I gave him the dirtiest look and said the buses don't run on Sunday. He laughed and said, take the car. I looked at him and said funny; you know you took the keys. He said what are you talking about and walked over to the key holder and there were my keys. The car keys swung from his hand. He looks at me and says are you alright and makes the crazy finger around the head signal. I wanted to smack his teeth straight out of his mouth. I just looked and said, ok.

In my mind I was thinking this motherfucker is trying to gaslight me!?? what the fuck!? I'm crazy?! Right. I grabbed the keys and got ready to take my grandson to

Skokie Water Park. It felt surreal. I was watching myself watch my grandson. Trying so hard to appear fun thanking God he was enjoying himself. I was going to take him out to eat and apologize and tell him he had to go home. At the restaurant, I brought up Midnight and said I didn't like the way he was acting so I have to get rid of him before you could stay. He asked why doesn't he just leave? I said I don't know and left it at that. I promised him I'd pick him back up as soon as I could churning with more anger as I realize this jackass was ruining the beginning of my grandsons' vacation! We'd go home and get his stuff, and I'd take him back home.

That didn't work out that Sunday. Of course, he needed the van! He never did go anywhere. I asked him that night calmly why don't you just leave. You're making this worse. I am not going to have any discussions with my grandson here and you acting like a total jerk. He said I will when I'm ready and smiled. Again, I wanted to smack that smile off his face. I no longer saw him the same. He was a stranger that could hurt my grandson or me. I'd kill him first was my thought.

The next day was supposed to be the usual. We shared a van, I dropped him off and took off to my job, because I work at more than one location. I would then pick him up when he got off of work. Well, he decides that morning that he is taking the van because he has to attend training. I was in no way arguing with this fool at 6 am, still had my grandson with me and had to figure out how to get to work and get him home. I was beyond frustrated already! Monday, June 25th. I decided to cancel my first Fitness class of the day because working with pace, a 30-minute ride becomes and an hour and 45 minutes on timed buses and I didn't have enough time to arrive on time. I focused on changing my mood and got my grandson up, made him breakfast, and prepared to bus it to my next location. Thank God I had just one other class scheduled that day. A 20-minute drive would turn into an hour and a half.

Well, the sunshine that is my oldest grandson took me right out of that fuck mode to which I had begun my day with. We read on the bus and laughed, and he sat in my Zumba gold class, while I got my happy on! It was a beautiful sunny day! We went home to peace and quiet, and upon entering the house, I noticed the vibe without Midnight there was totally different. Totally. I dismissed it and put attention back to my grandson, and we decided to play outside. We grabbed his scooter and bubbles, of course, and chose to play in the courtyard since just about everything was a reasonable distance to walk to. The afternoon was peaceful and fun while I thought Murphy's law is always consistent. I asked my grandsons Mom to pick him up, but their car had broken down. I looked up the bus schedule, and it would take 2 hours to take him home on public transportation. The thought of 4 hours travel time was terrible, but not as horrendous as the sick feeling in my gut I'd had all day that something was going to happen. Something was very wrong.

As we played outside, other kids in the courtyard started coming out to join us. I let my grandson continue to play with five other kids while I walked around with our dog, and he got snuggles and love from the crew, as I called them.

I recall my grandson saying oh, oh, look who's here, and I looked in the direction he was looking, and Midnight was coming from work. All smiles, waving at us. He even told the kids to catch as he flung a purple frisbee their way.

My stomach felt sicker, seeing his phony smile and demeanor. I did not smile back, I just looked thinking why the fuck didn't you just stay away. More sickening was my grandson's reaction to him. It didn't matter what he did or didn't hear, I know he felt that shitty vibe that man was emitting. I thought oh fuck, I'm going to get ready to try to get my grandson home. I didn't even want a conversation. I couldn't believe he pulled that bullshit this morning. His van now.

After a while, I decided to have my grandson go inside, clean up, eat, and we were going to head out. He wasn't pleased, but I promised him, I'd get him as soon as we got our house back all for us. And Scooby too, he added. We went inside the house, and it smelled marvelous. Midnight had come in and cooked up a storm. How narcissistically lovely of him. He says Gabriel you want some pork chops. He said yes, his favorite. So, I served my grandson and held the urge to barf on him and his food. While he was eating, I was getting ready for us to leave and had my bus pass on the table. He asked, where are you going? I said, I have to take Gabriel home. He asked, on the bus? I said yes since you want to dictate the use of the car. He said, see that's your problem, you're so dramatic over nothing.

Take the car, I didn't tell you can't use it. In my head, it was all kinds of what the fuck? I didn't even dispute his bullshit. I hustled and got the fuck out of there to take my grandson home.

By the time I made it back home it was about 10 pm, and he was sprawled on the sofa. I went over and sat next to him, and he looked over and said, what did I have under my eyes. I said sadness. He said don't be sad, I mentioned how could I not be when you're acting like such a cruel person towards me.

What the fuck is wrong with you? He said, oh this again! I said, why don't you just leave? It was about the third time in as many days I asked him to leave. He said when I get everything straight, I'll go. I said no. Am I just supposed to put up with your vicious self? He said to take it as you want, now leave me the fuck alone. I got up and went to bed and decided the next day I would get him the fuck out of my house.

It was Tuesday, 6/26/2018, a beautiful sunny summer day. A day I was sure we would both remember forever.

Despite his grouchy ass, I managed to find joy and gratitude in what I had. It bothered him. "What are you so happy about"? I didn't even respond. Hurry up, don't make us late! As if I ever! I still didn't respond. I felt sick to my stomach! I knew it was his dead mothers' birthday, and he tended to be extra sullen, whatever the fuck that meant. I kept thinking about getting the restraining order, and maybe he would just leave if I asked one more time. My mind was battling itself responding… you asked three days in a row. Almost begged him to leave and he laughed in your face. I'll leave when I'm ready! What a rat bastard he turned out to be! I was stunned at his behavior! Oh, don't act like you didn't fight with other boyfriends! I looked him dead in the eye and said if there ever was one, that was the end of us. I don't do the fighting game. I was ready to drop him off and drive myself to work as usual. It was Tuesday, and I had to pick him up at 3:00 pm. He said I'll drive as we exited the house and walked towards the driver's side of the van.

I got in the car thankful I had my headphones in my bag. I could feel the putrid hate oozing from this man. I was beyond disgusted. I don't know why it changed so drastically, but I could not have this man in my house any longer. I had to get rid of him. He was being arrogant, talking about don't be late to pick me up while he was speeding. What do you have to do after class? I said I had an appointment right after. He said, just don't be late. I said yesm bosem. He looked at me as he drove and said I'll throw you right out of this car and then you could figure out with your smart-ass mouth how you going to get to work! I was amazed. I just looked at him dead in the eye while I pulled my headphones out of my bag and was done with hearing him! He laughed mockingly. Did I hurt your feelings? Laughing menacingly! I hated him so much at that moment. I couldn't believe he was the same man I thought I adored. No fucken way in the world, I thought! I thought of canceling my afternoon and going to the Skokie courthouse. I needed him out. The information the sheriff gave us ran thru my mind…

He pulled into Graham gas station on Dempster and said I'll be back. Not if I want anything, you ok? Nothing. All of a sudden, I thought his keys! I didn't realize how badly my hands were shaking until I saw them before me fumbling to remove the two house keys from his keychain not even thinking, what if he noticed? I was laser-focused looking up and down to see if he was still inside. I managed to pull them off the keychain and put them in my pocket, just as the convenience store door opened and he strolled proudly to the car. I turned and looked out the window holding my hands together to keep them from shaking…

He jumped in the car proceeded to drive himself to work. As he exited the van and I took the driver's seat, he looked at me as if I was a child. 3 pm, don't be late! He said with the most sarcasm and grizzly smile ever. Have a nice day. I looked at him, rolled down the window, and told him, oh I will. I don't know about you and drove off to teach my Zumba class.

I pulled over down the street to calm down! I texted him, thanks for the life lesson, may God help you! As I drove the short distance, my mind was going crazy and thinking of the cruel things he had said all throughout the weekend! Called the sheriff on me! What a fucken mockery! I kept thinking; I don't want to do this!

I arrived at my class and told a close friend, Nadine, about getting a restraining order because he wouldn't leave and is being vicious! Do what you gotta do, she said. The only person I breathed a word to. I was so conflicted in my head! That morning before I finished my class, my Zumba sister, Bianca and her son Geo were coming to camp at the location where I taught! I got such big hugs as the doubt of whether I should go to get the order or not came to a halt and I decided to see them as a sign to go! After class, my friend wished me luck and told me she'd be there for me. I love Nadine; she always has been there for me!

I rushed home, my hands still shaking. I ran in the house, let the dog out really fast and came back in. The house was still. I could feel the entire shift of energy now that he wasn't present. I was stunned at the malice I realized he had. I rushed into action now angry and started taking all his shit and putting it in garbage bags! I packed everything that he had! I loaded the two garbage bags in the middle of the living room, and it was time for the 20-minute ride to the Skokie courthouse. The thought made me want to vomit. My hands could not stop shaking. All I reminded myself is how he had grabbed me for the first and last time two days before. I had taken pictures of a bruised leg and arm thanks to him, putting his hands on me. I was so nervous it took three attempts to find the parking lot to a place I had previous trauma, over in the past. When I finally found parking, I felt I was going to throw up! I had been there before, and those memories flooded me along with the sense of disbelief that I had to put this man out of my house because he wouldn't leave. What a fucken pussy I picked!

I finally got the courage to go in and pass thru metal detectors, directions, and waves of nausea. I remember thinking of Wonder Woman and her warrior status and recall walking in with clenched fists standing tall, terrified, but ready to do this.

I found the information desk, and they proceeded to direct me to some help on an upper floor. I almost passed out when I got this booklet of an application. No one was free because they had appointments, so the best they could do is explain to me that I had to fill out this booklet of paperwork and to not leave any blanks.

If I wanted an order today, I had to file before 1:30 pm. I believe it was for the court at 2:30 pm. I recall it was less than an hour, and I was feeling panic as bile rose to my throat.

The volunteer noticed, and she directed me to a desk in a section where I could have privacy and said, "just take your time." I said ok, but in my mind, I thought I can't take my time! I want this morning to be the last time that man was in my home! I couldn't wait for another day. My heart was pounding, my mouth was dry, and I thought how the fuck am I going to get these shaking fingers to fill out this packet! I sat down and started deep breathing because I was ready to pass out. I'm filling out the paperwork, and I hear a text notification. When I check, Midnight said I'm getting out early! I froze! I couldn't stop looking at the message! My hands shook even more as I clasped the phone. Oh, fuck! An hour and a half earlier! Murphys Law! You-Fucken ass hat!!! I didn't respond right away, thinking about what the fuck do I do!?? I went back to filling out the forms and my mind was racing; working so hard to focus! Reading and rereading the questions and then my responses! Though my phone was on silent, I could see the light repeatedly as he kept calling. He began to text, answer the phone, where are you? I texted I was at an appointment and he'd have to wait. He said he'd meet me at Golf Mill. I said, ok. I furiously went back to filling out the forms; so many thoughts running thru my head! I hated him for making me feel this frantic over this situation. I had to literally use breaths while I tried to calm down. I started to pay attention and saw an area where I could list the van in the order until I figured out what to do. I put the television on as well just to be a bitch really, I didn't give a fuck about this big ass tv, but he did. I went filed the order; I believe they waved the fee because I don't recall paying, but so much happened! I barely made it in time to see the judge that afternoon! I had to wait for about 30 minutes. Meanwhile, he texted, where are you?

This is fucked up, so very typical, you will need it again; (referring to the van he decided to say was only his now!) where are you?

I sent bullshit texts, no games, where are you at? I have the keys; the windows are closed! Ok, I need something from the store. We could talk then and see what you are going to do; I'm tired. All bullshit, while I waited to see if I would be given a restraining order that day. When I was finally called, the judge asked why I wanted the order.

I began by telling her about Sunday and showing her, as I pulled my sleeve up, two days later, still purple where Midnight had grabbed my arm viciously for the first and last time. I told the judge how he stated he'd throw me out of the car that morning . I told her about how he said he'd tear my house up. I told her how he told my grandson the two days before to jump off the roof, "and then you'll learn about gravity." I told her a shitload of things that happened in the past four days, and as my voice shook, I had to pause several times to keep from totally screaming and crying; but I answered all questions. In the end, that judge saw enough reasons to grant a restraining order.

Now I had to go to the sheriff to serve it and get him out! I wanted so desperately for him not to reenter the house. At this point, he stopped responding to my texts. He must've realized he didn't' have the keys once he got there! Is he in the house? How did he get in? So many questions! My brain was exploding! I waited for the paperwork and asked how to do this. The sheriff was right next to the complex I live at. They could serve him, and I was free.

It was the first moment I thought about how this mother fucker made me feel caged this weekend. Up against a wall. I don't do well that way. I need to get free.

I jumped in my car and started making my way home. The sheriff is next to the complex, but I had no idea where the entrance was! I remember trying to find the entrance, failing, and having the young man at the front desk call to meet me. I went outside and drove to the entrance of my complex and said I'd be waiting there and told them the color of the van. I stated I didn't know if he was in the house. If he was, he broke in. He had no keys.

Two sheriffs, a man, and a woman met me, and I proceeded to explain the situation and show them the paperwork. The woman looked truly bothered. The man was more sympathetic. I don't know why, but I certainly felt the bias. The woman said I don't think we can do this. For one moment, my stomach dropped. The man responded; no, we have jurisdiction to do this.

I said, please and get the copy of the van key and I showed them where the van was listed on the order. I told them I had a pit bull and to ask him to put him in the bedroom and close the door. I also gave the sheriffs a bus pass that had $3. I said give him this. He's broke. It was the last nice thing I would ever do for him.

I went back to the van, nervously waiting for this part to pass. It felt like an eternity. More like 30 - 40 minutes. They said he's gone, and I said thank you. I jumped in the van and drove home. I could see my back door open as I entered, and my neighbor came out. She was concerned and asked her son to go in my apartment because she didn't see me. She saw the sheriff leave with Midnight and was concerned. I told them what happened and if they ever saw him to, please call the police or call me, and I gave them my cell. I said I would tell the other neighbors and workers as well. I walked into my house, looking around. The two garbage bags were just as I left them. I grabbed them and took them out to the van. I wanted them out of my sight! I looked around, feeling something was wrong and BINGO! My brand-new tablet I had just purchased for myself a few days before, was gone! I left it charging! Charger and all were gone! This motherfucker stole my tablet! Now we were on a whole other level! I got even more furious! I went outside to see how he got in. Took pictures of the screen and window, he left fucked up. I fixed it and then went inside, and with much effort pushed a large armoire in front of the window in my bedroom.

"Return the tablet tonight, I won't add burglary charges" I said to his daughters and told them what he had done. I gave them until the following day to contact him and return my tablet.

This motherfucker was never going to be able to get in thru that window again! I was furious and messaged his daughters that I was going to add theft if I didn't get that tablet back in 24 hours! I couldn't believe he stole from me. I had been nothing but good to that man. We were friends long before. Or so I thought…My adrenaline was pumping, and I was so mad about the theft, having him removed hadn't sunk in yet! The sheriff threw him out! My space was safe again! But it felt tainted. I looked around and hated everything about it. I had to stop myself and remember to be grateful. He was out of my house. My home. The beginning of him being out of my life. The beginning of removing his stench from my soul.

I took a shower and became obsessed with changing how the furniture was set. I couldn't remove the picture of him on it. I hated the image. It made me cry and get furious. How could he try to treat me like I was going to support his abuse? What the fuck! I was dumbfounded. I felt stupid and ashamed being involved in this ghetto soap opera. I hated him for bringing this experience upon me. Why couldn't he just leave!?? Why did he have to act like he could stay and talk to me that way? What the fuck was he thinking?!! I changed my living room, attempting to purge the stench of him from my life.

The next morning, I let the sunshine in, the freedom. The lightness I felt carry me thru the sadness I felt in my crushed heart. I had an outdoor water fitness class. Perfect. No one knew a thing about anything. I don't know why. At the time, I didn't even think of calling anyone. I was too shocked that I was in that situation. I cried all the time. I wanted to be alone.

IT HURTS

For months, I would look at our names on that restraining order in disbelief! Months do you hear me? I hadn't seen this man before the last three years for maybe eight years, but we worked together and played together for years! I had been around this man the previous three years, and he had never so much as raised his voice. We talked out our problems, children, drank together, cooked together, laughed a lot together. He had massaged my hurting legs endlessly.

Who the fuck was this man I had thrown out? He was very vicious looking, menacing, meanness from every pore… I carried on teaching my classes and babysitting as if nothing had happened. My friend Nadine gave me high praises and said I was brave. Although I cried every night, I spoke to no one. It was something I wanted to wash off my soul. The hurt was so much. I adored her support.

The day after court, three weeks later, I group messaged some supportive ladies I know and let them know what had happened. They showered me with support as I cried uncontrollably from my end, thanking God for such good people when I felt diminished. I later spoke to my friend Marina about the incident. I remember I didn't cry; I was angry. Angry, he would dare be so mean and expect me to do nothing. He stole my tablet to take anything! I had supported this man in every way, never did a bad thing to him. I was beyond hurt and disgusted. It wasn't a matter of please stay; it was why motherfucker.

I later found out he moved from my house to his current love interests' home. More confirmation this man was nothing but deceitful. He had actually introduced this woman to me as his friend. What a disgusting piece of low life!

I thought in talking to my friend about the ordeal, I would be done with this bullshit to move on and forget all about this rat bastard. It wasn't that simple...

There was a three-week waiting period until the court date to determine if the order would stay in place. It allowed him to defend himself. I so hoped he just wouldn't show up. Just let me keep the van and get out of my life.

I expressed how disgusted I was that he could do such a thing to someone that had always had his back. His oldest daughter, 25 years old, was so relaxed about the situation. I knew this wasn't new to her. "I wish you guys were still in love and happy! Oh well, maybe my dad will get it together when he's 60". His behavior turned out to be new only to me. His family loved him from a distance because of this very behavior. I was stunned.

His oldest daughter begged me not to make a police report she would get the tablet. The result? He sent the message thru his daughters for me to go to Maywood and pick up my tablet. My rage was unprecedented. I was screaming, cursing in my house. How dare he!? I thought. The restraining order would be null and void if I did that. Clearly, he thought I was an idiot. Or he was. I filed a police report.

Messages from his daughters were confirmation that he had stolen it because he wasn't seen. I just know the last person in the house was him before the sheriffs threw him out. I know he was shocked. I know he didn't expect it from me. I know it still didn't sink into him that I had an order of protection. I also had possession of the van he had taken back, so I had at least three weeks to keep it until the judge ruled who got to keep it. It was in both our names.

In the three weeks to come, I cried so much in a rage that he could mistreat me and expect me to take it. That he didn't want to leave and was so mocking and condescending. That he would dare speak to a little boy, my little boy no less with such malice and not expect me to flip. Fucken idiot never knew me then. The last message I sent him on Facebook before he blocked me was the day he was removed from my house. It was 5:52 pm, "Good luck. You should've respected me. "I had hate and rage, and it scared me. I had never felt such anger at a situation. Ever.

Humiliation, insult, disbelief, rage, all bad things were flowing through me. I pretty much stayed away from everyone.   I could recall picking my grandson up the following week. That night as we talked in bed in the dark looking at our glow in the dark stars, I'll never forget my grandson saying. Lola even the stars are brighter since Midnight is gone" I was stunned and told him you are so right my love. I had to speak to my grandson about that whole situation and about what I don't tolerate and how he would never see Midnight in this house again.

COURT DATE

I will never forget that Wed, July 18th, 1:30 pm.

I had hoped he wouldn't show up, but my gut was telling me he was coming for the van. He had bought it for me, but I bet that story would change once he was in front of the judge. I went early to the courthouse. My stomach sick with not knowing what would happen. I had decided if he showed up, he could have the van back, my car was finally fixed. I didn't need two cars. I knew he would need a car. I recall being on the 2nd floor of the courthouse, and suddenly I felt ice cold and looked down towards the entrance. There he was in a violet-blue shirt that looked stunning against his dark skin. I was disgusted, and I moved back when he looked up so he wouldn't see me. My body turned to ice; I could feel my frozen hands. They would remain so until I got home.

I followed him with my eyes in disbelief that I was a significant part of what I considered a ghetto soap opera. I hated it so much. I decided to stay on the 2nd floor wondering if it was worth trying to talk to him before court began to let him know to take the van; your shit is in it and never speak to me again. That's not what happened. At one point, while waiting for the time to be in front of the judge, I needed to use the restroom. He came out of nowhere! He saw me and immediately made as if he was scared, arms flailing, laughing mocking me. This was funny to him. I was instantly filled with more rage and decided I would not offer the van. I would let the judge decide. He was so childish and idiotic to make those gestures. My only reaction, I stopped made sure he was looking right at my face and held up my hand wait, nodded, and turned away. I went and changed the paperwork and put the van back for possession.

I could recall the dryness of my mouth to have to be in such close proximity to this man. The room where we waited for the judge felt small to me. He sat two rows ahead of me. He had shiny new black shoes, black pants, and that shocking violet shirt. He looked very handsome until you looked in his eyes. I could tell he had gone back to full-fledged drinking, his face had breakouts and his eyes were so yellow that day. He looked at me with a mocking look. I hated him so much that day. I wanted to slap the mocking look off of his face. I wanted to throw up; I felt so ill at him even looking at me. Turns out he wasn't served the correct papers, to which they served him in court. We took a recess to see if he wanted to continue or answer now. He chose now. In the time until court readjourned, I jumped out of my seat desperate to not be in the same room as that man. He felt so hateful to me. I couldn't believe we were there.

Our turn finally came. He stood right next to me as I looked at him. I was beyond disgusted. I didn't want to stand anywhere near him. I could recall looking him up and down and thinking, never can a motherfucker get away with treating me like he did.

He looked tainted. He looked ashy to me, even though his hair was short, it looked dirty. His eyes had so much red and yellow in them. I wonder if he was already drinking. I could feel the hatred emanating from him. Ugh, I didn't want to stand this close. I instantly became nauseous. Like pregnant nausea, like give me some deep breaths nauseous. I went alone. I don't know why. I know a handful of women who would've gladly accompanied me. Maybe it's because I just didn't want to repeat the story.

Months later and I still have difficulty writing it. The judge came in, and it began. I went first as he was asked to sit. We were told we could object and address the objection at the end. I described the weekend before the order. The abusive language towards me, the pictures of the bruises when he did grab me. The vicious remarks he had made within three days. Texts for proof. I was asked questions by the judge as I heard my voice not sounding like my voice. Strained and low. Steady but low. Loud enough to hear, but flat, full of anger. I'm never low.

When it was his turn, it was showtime. I suddenly saw the act that he put on for the world regularly. "I'm an educator; I love kids. I've been doing this for over 25 years. I can't have a restraining order on my record. She's the abusive one."

I objected repeatedly and later told the judge how he said, "I work with kids all day. I don't want to see any on the weekend." Just kidding. He wasn't joking. He did not like to be around children at all. Maybe because in his heart, he knows how malicious he is. He brought up how he cooked for me all the time, massaged my legs. Yes, he did cook for me, but it was more for him than me. He did massage my legs when I was in pain. I can't explain that humane act. An anomaly of what he had become.

I was astounded as he told the judge he had to call 911 because I attacked him with a lit cigar. He said I smashed it in his face while he was sleeping. I was stunned and more mortified, and I didn't think that was possible. He said I was consistently abusive and locked him out that was against the law. I stole his house keys. He said that the van was his. That I didn't even know who he bought it from. All these were lies. Every single thing. He looked very dramatic this 6ft 9 man black as coal with a violet shirt. Tried to shine like a penny, but his tarnished ways were so evident. I was sitting thinking omg what if they believe him!? WTF! When I responded I told the judge, if I touched him, he would be showing you the scars.

Deep inside, I kept thinking of how I busted his lip that sat night. I wasn't going to bring it up! I assaulted him for calling me a hoe. It was never discussed in court. He went on and on of how I always fought with him and sent him mean messages, but the only proof he had was a message I had sent the last weekend, stating that now I knew he wasn't what I thought. He was vicious and mean, and I wanted him gone. The judge saw nothing abusive about that. She was telling you about yourself, was her understanding. He said his phone was stolen because he was staying here and there. The "Poor me" act. He even name-dropped Gene Moores' funeral he had attended. So grandiose.

I explained to the judge; he bought me the van when my car was broken down than his truck broke down. Then he decided to take the van back when he turned abusive. I was stunned at all the lies he said about me.

We took a break, then the judge would rule. I wanted him never to contact me again. Seeing him that day showed me I did not know this man. I thought we were friends, but even that was a lie. I immediately left the courtroom to escape his funky vibe. I would not reenter until we reconvened. I could see him looking at me from inside the courtroom. I gave him the most stank eye I could muster. I hated him so much, his lies, his arrogance.

When we reconvened, the judge said she had enough evidence to grant the order and asked me how long. Forever! People laughed; I was serious. She said orders are only for two years, let's do 1. Whatever I just wanted it permanent.

I was disgusted at everything that came into question over this relationship. I felt everything was a big ass lie. I stated if someone did what he did to me to one of his daughters, he'd go nuts. He immediately agreed with it and realized afterward what a jackass he just made of himself by saying, "hell yeah!" while in court !

The judge granted me one year of a restraining order, he was to get his clothes and TV, return the tablet, and the judge gave me the van. I was thrilled! I could see the shock on his face, and he kept saying, what? Wow, wow, you are going to give her my van? The judge told him to be silent before she held him in contempt.

Great moment. Glorious!

Midnight had one week to pick his stuff up and return my stolen tablet.

On Sunday, 6/22/18 three years later to the date, this man sought me out, he came and picked his stuff up. I was so apprehensive wanting it over. Thinking all of him will finally be gone! His daughters' God sister and someone named Butch came.

They couldn't understand my rage. I had placed all his belongings in garbage bags and kept them in my van. He had a large TV to take as well. As they took the bags,

I see a white truck passing slowly, and it was him! How fucken dare he come here!? I screamed, what the fuck is he doing here! He knows damn well I have a restraining order! This was the moment his family found out about the restraining order. I will call the sheriff right now! His family stated; they had no idea. Big surprise!! He wasn't smirking this day. Serious. They took his belongings and returned my tablet. He tried to give it without the charger, and I said no TV, suddenly the charger showed up.

Dirty til the bitter end. I was livid!! I went inside and took a shot of whiskey! I recalled how I had poured syrup and ketchup on some of his belongings two weeks before. Petty, but satisfying.

Two days later, on July 24, 2018, at 11:07 pm, I received a message. "Eat a thousand rotten dick's "Midnight sent thru YouTube. I responded by sending him a Cardi B video, Be careful and two emojis. First with sunglasses, Second with a wink. I messaged and said if he ever contacts me again, I'll enforce the restraining order.

He was shocked. I'm sure he was in Maywood working in Rogers Park with no car. He got what he deserved. He should've been fined too for daring to touch me. I don't give a fuck if it was once. The judge gave him one week to pick his stuff up. I would coordinate with his oldest daughter as he'd traumatized the youngest pregnant one with this ordeal already. I left that courthouse filled with victory, but still full of rage. I don't think I fully appreciated one because of the other at the time.

Before I left the courthouse, I bumped into the same sheriff who had been called on me that Sunday. I stopped and thanked him for the information. He asked if I was ok. I said if you ever see that guy arrest him, I have a restraining order and I don't plan to rescind it. He said good for you and wished me luck. Great feeling. Of all the sheriffs to run into in such a vast place! I did feel victorious. I felt like I had just dropped kicked this fool and it was glorious!!!

I went home, and my heart was still pounding. I couldn't believe I had really won! It was so scary. I cried from relief and stress and how the fuck could he!?? There was still one part left. He had one week to pick up his stuff, return the tablet he stole and give me the copy of the van keys. I tried to keep his TV, which I had also put on the order out of pettiness because I knew he loved it. The judge said no he bought it before we lived together, which was just fine. I was ecstatic! She awarded me the van and demanded he return my tablet undamaged. It was new; I hadn't even had a chance to use it! I had already packed everything and put it out in the van.

In the 1st week after the emergency restraining order, I brought the clothes back in the house when I had too much time to think and act petty. I couldn't stop thinking of the situation in total disbelief. I thought we were friends. It was one of the last things I said to that man. I was hurt and not mad. I was in a rage that he

would grab me as he did over keys, that he would lie as he did. That he would be so hateful when all I had ever done was love and support him.

Two weeks prior, I took seven of his favorite shirts. I washed them and put them in my car and gave them to men on the streets one by one. Gave me immense satisfaction. I took his favorite jeans threw them in the trash, a jacket he wore for a graduation we attended together donated it to an employment program for men along with two dress shirts. I threw away one gym shoe, I threw one flip flop away, poked a hole in his winter boots, put syrup inside a hat, put hot sauce on a favorite dress shirt and took two African shirts which he loved so much. I took one shirt and ripped it from rage. I later took the shirt and refashioned a little stool with it to combat my negative feelings. That gave me great satisfaction.

I did it all at the moment because I was hurt, in disbelief, in rage. I had three weeks until the order was finalized, and I felt impatient. I had to stop myself and think I am not going to let him drive me to be something or someone I'm not. That was how I expressed my rage.

I kept to myself.

I remember the evening he was thrown out. I changed the entire living room. I couldn't stand the images that haunted my mind, so I tried to change the visual. It was such a horrible feeling. The night I got the restraining order, I changed the entire living room again.... getting up the next morning reminded me of why I changed it. I wanted to burn my bed, discard all the good memories that interrupted my pain. I could no longer go to sleep with YouTube and those loving love songs. It disgusted me. This was when I began sleeping with meditation music or abundance music.

It was December 2018, six months after this bullshit and I thought I was over it. I had written several poems spitting my rage. I started a Facebook page for myself. I told no one. I needed no validation at all. I was letting out my anger slowly. The taste was beyond bitter.

It's April 2019, and I've just started to listen to the songs I loved so much, and I love them again. My mindset when I heard a song that reminded me of Midnight Madness would be one day someone is going to sing those songs and mean them this time. I refused to let him taint what I loved so much.

A lovely woman started a publishing company that was supposed to be for me. I needed to write to heal. It was on a video chat with other authors that I really "saw" my rage and hate and hurt. It was horrible.

I FORGIVE MYSELF

I am relieved. I no longer feel that way.

I ask myself; do I forgive him? Some days no, most days, yes.

All that ordeal was about him. I am still learning about paths and not being ashamed of the bullshit life throws our way. I am just going to have to be a Bullshit Beat Down Babe.

I never expected, going thru the very thing, that filled me with hate and would empty me of the vileness of it all. To feel relieved and see things as they were. To forgive myself and remember that all I did for that man was out of love. When I had him thrown out, that love was for me. I still believe in love. I see examples of it, and I refuse to let a narcissistic asshole experience change that. I want that love, crazy, unconditional -I love you even on your bad days love. It's out there.

As I sit getting myself together, I recall that broken people bleed on others. I refuse to be that person.

It's been ten months. He has never contacted me again.

I FORGIVE YOU

Dear Jerry,

I want you to know that I forgive you. More importantly, I forgive myself.

The experience of you having abused me forced me to recognize a strength I had no idea I had. I had to look at the fact that just because you weren't beating me, didn't mean you weren't abusing me.

Verbal and emotional abuse is not being addressed, and it's happening so much. It will NEVER be the norm for me. The situation you put me in made me go thru a rage I've never experienced before. It was dark, ugly, and scary. I cried constantly. I wanted to be alone. I had physical pain and couldn't sleep. I was having such a difficult time writing about it. I was told it would help me heal. I was doubtful. I was beyond mad. Rage. Blind Rage. I would get into such a fit of rage; I amazed myself. I was angry at you and mad at myself. I felt stupid and used. I felt humiliated over the entire process I had to endure to get you out. It did help me heal.

My publisher suggested picturing you as a child, and that is what ultimately helped me immerse myself in the reliving and writing of this story — imagining you as a child made me recall how you were abused for so many years. My heart would melt at the thought. I would remind myself why I fell in love with you; recall the silver lining in you. The meals cooked and the many hours of leg massages and I knew all of it wasn't an act. I would recall all the years we were friends and supported each other.

Writing about this experience made me face the shame, the pain, the bullshit remarks of, he only grabbed you once! It was like having to go thru the darkest of places, with putridness and suffering everywhere, but if I didn't, I would never be free of the pain you caused me. I realized it was a story of betrayal.

I trusted you as my friend and then my boyfriend for many years. I thought I knew you. You didn't let all of you be known.

My publisher went thru years of emotional abuse and talking to her several times thru tears of rage and shame helped me to move my story along. Letting me talk it out and validating the fact that verbal abuse is still abuse.

I threw you out because I loved me more. Looking back, I can't believe I wrote this book in under six months.

You need to revisit your story. Deal with your pain and shame and all the things it has caused you even now in your 50's. There is good in you. Start with the inside —

that silver lining you choose to show people. There is a pain in you, you disregard, and it's ruined you and caused you to hurt the ones that loved you the most.

I don't regret anything about us or anything I did for you. That was love. Despite your imperfections, I had immense love for you. You knew it, and you used it. Love is tolerant, not blind. Abuse is not love. There's a lot of self-hate in it. You're a smart man. Your daughter said it well," Until my Daddy heals himself, he will hurt every woman he is with." Heal yourself. Your family loves you. Stop displaying the narcissistic duplicity.

I wish you peace, love, and progress in your life. It was a life-changing experience to cross paths again.

Midnight is dead. Goodbye Jerry.

Debbie

STEPS FOR SECURING A RESTRAINING ORDER

Go to the courthouse (ask for advocates - many times it's free to assist with direction)

Fill out the paperwork they give you.
Slow down, be thorough.
Ask for an emergency restraining order.
Write down the things you most want the judge to know.
Put down anything you think he may want to take in the interim. I waited three weeks until court, and I placed a van that was under both names on the restraining order. The judge then decides who keeps the car or whatever you put on the sheet.
You can also include wanting them to stay away from children or family members that may be subject to retaliation.

After all the paperwork is filled out check if advocates can make sure you have all filled out correctly. If no one available go thru all sheets once more.

When complete go, file the papers with the clerk.

For emergency orders to be given, you have to meet time deadlines. I caught the last one of the day. 1:30 pm. I saw the judge at 3 pm, by 5 pm I had an emergency restraining order.

The sheriff or police can then serve the abuser and be escorted out of your residence.

There will be a court date when it will be determined if the order will stand and the person can come and defend themselves.

When the court date comes, expect to stand before the judge next to your abuser. Write things down on index cards.

Bring a friend. I knew I'd get nervous, dry mouth. It was terrifying and disgusting all at once. Don't go through this alone.

A determination will be made that day.

Domestic Abuse Hotline: 1-800-799-7233

There are also shelters available that house pets as well.

There are online chats available for support.

Check your local community agencies and churches for assistance.

Stay strong and remember, you deserve better than this.

www.ingramcontent.com/pod-product-compliance
Lightning Source LLC
Chambersburg PA
CBHW020008290326
41935CB00007B/347